Time
for Us

Time for Us

RICHARD J. BECKMEN

THOMAS NELSON PUBLISHERS
Nashville

Published in Nashville, Tennessee, by Oliver-Nelson Books, a division of Thomas Nelson, Inc., Publishers, and distributed in Canada by Word Communications, Ltd., Richmond, British Columbia.

The Bible version used in this publication is THE NEW KING JAMES VERSION. Copyright © 1979, 1980, 1982, Thomas Nelson, Inc., Publishers.

Scripture quotations noted NRSV are from the New Revised Standard Version of the Bible. Copyright © 1989 by the Division of Christian Education of the National Council of the Churches of Christ in the United States of America.

"Turn Your Eyes Upon Jesus" by Helen H. Lemmel copyright © 1922 Singspiration Music/ASCAP. All rights reserved. Used by permission of Benson Music Group, Inc.

Printed in the United States of America.

Library of Congress Cataloging-in-Publication Data

Beckmen, Richard J.
     Time for us / Richard J. Beckmen.
          p.   cm.
     Includes bibliographical references.
     ISBN 0-8407-9189-5
     1. Married people—Prayer-books and devotions—English.
2. Spiritual journals—Authorship.   I. Title.
BV4596.M3B43   1993
242'.644—dc20   93-6666
                                                                              CIP

1 2 3 4 5 6 — 98 97 96 95 94 93

To Solveig

Companion and friend
on the journey
to spiritual intimacy

Contents

INTRODUCTION

*T*his book has one basic purpose—to lead you and your spouse on a common journey of spiritual intimacy. Jesus' promise to be present with us is the basis of an expectation you can have in experiencing God in your life together: "Where two or three are gathered together in My name, I am there in the midst of them" (Matt. 18:20). This journey will take you to a space and time that will allow you to share an experience of God's love moving within and between you.

Growth in the spiritual dimension of your relationship has two general areas—outer and inner. The outer dimension of your spiritual growth consists of worship services, Bible reading and study, caring acts for others, and concern for justice. This expression of religious activity in the outer world is a basic aspect of spiritual development.

However, outward expressions are not the only concern. Your spiritual growth as individuals and as a couple has an inner dimension. This inward movement toward God is related to silence, contemplation, and a shared experience of realizing God's presence within and between you. The movement toward God is an experience similar to your falling in love with each other. In marriage you seek a coming together that takes a lifetime to happen. This little book will suggest some ways to make that coming together be a part of your spiritual journey.

Jesus made a promise to be in the midst of every community that met in His name. In many respects your marriage is like a community. As you come together in making your marriage, you are building a community of shared life, love, and hope.

The way to build community in your marriage is to move together in prayer, shared silence in Jesus' presence, and growth in understanding the Scriptures.

The spiritual dimension is as vital as any other aspect of your marriage and—like the rent, taxes, and anniversaries—is not to be neglected. The promise of community is that more will happen with another than can happen by yourself. In God's presence, one plus one equals three; two plus two equals five. This is the arithmetic of spiritual intimacy.

It is not just a matter of sharing the same room, the same bed, the same dinner table, or the same money. Even if all of these things are shared, there can still be a great deal of loneliness and separateness.

At a workshop a woman mentioned to me that she had been lonely as a marriage partner and as a divorced person, but she would rather be lonely as a single person. If you have made a commitment to a relationship without pursuing intimacy, you will experience an increasing amount of loneliness.

You have committed yourself to the promise of growth through this relationship. Are you experiencing the fulfillment of that hope? You may end up with the taste of ashes in your mouth and the words of a familiar expression on your lips, "Is that all there is?" If you begin to occupy shared inner space together—shared thoughts, feelings, opinions, prayer, reflection, and silence in the presence of Christ—this loneliness does not need to happen.

BARRIERS TO INTIMACY

Various barriers can stifle attempts to get close to each other. This may be particularly true of spiritual intimacy.

Some have a fear that prevents them from seeking any kind of personal or interior experience of God. This fear may be caught up in the belief that God is primarily

Someone who spoils the fun you are having. God is perceived as a Being who does not like joy and is opposed to what is human. This fear may be rooted in wrong teaching or a lack of experience about the true nature of God. In Jesus, God is revealed as One who is seeking you to free and enable you to take part in great joy and freedom. This is the entire meaning of the forgiveness and love God extends to everyone in Christ. God is seeking fellowship with you as something to be enjoyed and celebrated.

Others avoid spiritual intimacy because they feel they do not know enough about the Bible, prayer, or the church. Such knowledge is a good thing but is not required for you to seek spiritual intimacy. God is willing to meet you where you are and to relate to you at whatever your stage of knowledge and experience. It is okay to begin at the beginning with God and with each other.

Just as individuals may experience difficulty in moving toward spiritual intimacy, so do some couples. One of you may have a strong background in prayer and spiritual discipline, and the other may be entering strange territory. In this case both need to acknowledge these issues and, for these shared times, be willing to proceed at a pace that is comfortable for both. Each of you will still have individual time for spiritual practices. This shared time is meant to help you grow toward each other in a mutual experience of God's presence.

You may have a strong background in individual prayer and reflection but not much experience in a shared practice of spirituality. You may come from a background where inner experiences of faith were not talked about very often. You may need to overcome initial embarrassment before you plunge in. Once you begin to share these experiences together, you will become more confident and eager.

Finally, realize that marriage has many challenges. Misunderstandings, deception, various acts of unconscious abuse, and false expectations may threaten the relationship. Illness, economic hardship, child rearing, and changing patterns in your adult lives may add considerable stress. These problems are not addressed directly in this book. Its purpose, rather, is to enable you to experience spiritual growth that will allow you to better face and solve these difficulties. It will provide a spiritual component to your relationship that will aid you in finding ways to meet stress and challenge.

This book is not a substitute for learning good communication and problem-solving skills. It should not allow you to hide from the emotional growth you need to experience.

Embarking on a shared inner journey of silence, prayer, and reflection may give you an awareness of parts of yourself and your partner that you will not appreciate. When you encounter these negative feelings about yourself or your partner, don't deny them, run away from them, or repress them. Acknowledge that they exist, accept them, and try to understand how you might live at peace with them. If you don't accept and work with these aspects of yourself and your partner, they will always hover over you as a dark shadow to create difficulties in your relationship.

Don't be discouraged by negative aspects in yourself or your partner. They point to growth and may, in time, become areas of strength and energy in your relationship as they become redeemed and redirected.

PERSONALITY AND PRAYER

Your personalities affect the way you pray. Each has unique aspects of personality. You may be quite different or somewhat similar. Individual personality types approach and experience prayer differently. An introverted person will find silence and solitude comfortable; an extroverted person may find that approach difficult. A thinking person may relate to prayer and spirituality more through the mind while a sensate person relates more through the world around. One is not necessarily better than the other. They are just different.

One of you may find the suggestions in this book very much to your liking. The other may not. Talk about and find ways to accommodate each other's spirituality.

Become aware of your particular way of praying. What feels natural and comfortable will be the easiest way for you to proceed. Share this method with your partner. If you would like to further explore this area of your prayer life, look in the recommended reading section at the end of this book.

SPIRITUALITY AND LIFE

There is a tendency you need to avoid in seeking to develop a shared spiritual journey. Our society tends to compartmentalize life, that is, to think of particular activities as separate and disconnected from other parts of life. Work, leisure, spirituality, and sexuality are activities that become isolated from one another. However, life is not that way. Our lives are really more of one piece than we think.

As you pursue this experiment in spirituality together, try not to think of it as something separate from other activities of your relationship. What happens with your spirituality will affect other aspects of your married life. For instance, spirituality and sexuality are often separated, but actually, they are very close together in human experience.

Many books on spirituality have been written by single and celibate persons. Sometimes their viewpoint toward sexuality is negative because they see it as something to overcome. It appears as an enemy to spirituality. However, for married persons, sexuality provides insight into intimacy and sharing that is relevant to understanding spirituality. Married persons do not need to perceive sexuality as something to be overcome or conquered. The sexual experience is at the very heart of marriage. What you learn of God, God's presence, and love ought to enhance and make more real and fulfilling your sexual experience as a couple.

This is just as true for other aspects of your life together, such as vacationing, working, planning, and talking. Your growth in spiritual awareness and discipline will begin to change, enhance, and deepen your other experiences; and those life experiences will begin to change, enhance, and deepen your spiritual awareness as well. You are an individual with many facets to your life, and they all interact. The point is to get them balanced and focused and working together in a positive way. Your spiritual life is most certainly a significant part of the picture and will contribute greatly to this balance and focus.

Pursuing a deepening of your spirituality will lead you more deeply into life. You and your spouse are joined together as two persons created in the image and out of the imagination of God. Who you are alone and who you are together are a part of God's plan. You have been created for relationship with God, alone and together. This book seeks to help you touch the edges of that reality by providing a disciplined opportunity to place yourselves where God can interact with your lives.

THE THIRTY-DAY EXPERIENCE

*T*his book presents thirty devotional exercises that can be shared in a common worship time. These exercises follow a simple yet definite pattern. They provide a framework in which both partners can explore a shared spiritual journey.

The book offers an outline and some suggestions for your silence, reflection, and prayer. However, you will bring your daily life experience into this shared worship time. The content of your devotional time needs to be shaped by the day you have lived, separately and together.

There may be a confession. There may be things to celebrate. There are thanks to be expressed for love given and received. There may be tears or smiles. There may be chores to share. There may be a need for some separate time or silence. It is most important for you to be real—real with God, with yourself, and with each other.

As you come together for your shared devotional time, be prepared to pray out of the experience of your day—feelings, thoughts, and needs. Let your real life at that moment flow into and out of your shared silence, your spoken words, your lived moments together.

Some days your devotional time will be exciting and rewarding. You will feel a strong awareness of God's presence as well as a lively sense of each other's presence. But there will be other days when the silence, the prayers, and the conversations will be flat, boring, and meaningless. Don't let the dry days cause you to give up. They are part of the natural rhythm of life. Keep at it. The energy and excitement of sharing this devotional time together will return. An individual's devotional life has creative and un-creative times. Your shared journey will be similar.

At times you will find each other at different places along the continuum of spiritual ups and downs. Go along with each other at this point, and try not to let one or the other of your moods dominate. For spiritual life to flourish, you don't need a lot of rules. Some days your shared time will be mostly touching. Other times it will be mostly talking or being silent. Let what seems to be important for that day take center stage in your relationship and your devotional life together. In being sensitive to God, yourself, and each other, you will be given the wisdom to know what is appropriate for that day and those moments.

DEVOTIONAL PATTERN

Here is the pattern for this devotional time together:
- Silence
- Scripture and Reflection
- Prayer
- Journaling
- Blessing

SILENCE

Begin each devotional time together with silence. At first the silence may seem awkward. The more you do it, the easier it will be. In this silence you seek detachment from preoccupations and concerns. You open to the presence of God. It helps to close your eyes and get into a comfortable position. Sit up straight with your legs un-crossed and your hands lying loosely in your lap. When you have found a comfortable position for your body, move inward.

This inward movement is a seeking after silence. It is like stripping a room bare. Eliminate the external light. Remove the furniture. Take down the pictures from the walls, and roll up the carpet on the floor. All these are distractions from just being. Forget what is outside, and make bare what is inside yourself for these moments.

When you go inward, you will discover mental distractions. Don't fight them. Let them come and then pass by. They will move on. If you allow yourself to dwell on these distractions, you will lose the inward movement.

Breathing becomes an important part of this process. In fact, breathing may be a way to assist your inward journey. As you become silent and still, be conscious of your breathing. Notice the rhythm. Focus on the breathing in and the breathing out. It is one way to get very still and avoid distractions. Don't force the rhythm of your breathing; follow it. Be conscious of the flow of air in and out.

Another help in making this silence meaningful is to use a single word or image. Repeat a significant word that will focus your mind and attention on God's presence. This word could be *God, Jesus, Holy Spirit, peace, love,* or another word that is essential to you as a symbol of the presence you seek. *This word is not a mantra.* You do not repeat it endlessly. You say it briefly until you are focused and still with the distractions put aside. If your mind wanders, go back and repeat the word a few times until you focus again.

In this quiet time you are seeking a few undistracted moments so that you will be open to receive what God and your partner may share with you. Too often we come to a devotional time so filled with distractions that we cannot get our minds off ourselves and on to another. In this practice you will not be seeking to avoid the day's feelings, frustrations, or concerns. They will come up in your sharing time. Focusing through silence will help you relate to what will come up in your discussions with a different perspective—a quiet mind and spirit.

These moments of shared silence are not just preparation for something else. They are important in themselves. The more you practice, the more you will begin to enjoy and be enriched by this quiet time. It will bring its own reward to your relationship.

Are you wondering if this silence is such a good thing because your relationship already has too much silence? Perhaps withdrawn and moody? This silence is chosen to lead to a connection with God and another, not separation. It is emptying yourself of negative thoughts and emotions so that you may be filled with God's renewing presence, peace, and harmony. This silence will enhance communication, not diminish it. Moreover, this type of silence is meant for letting go of control and being empty before God so that God can direct the thought and image. If you find yourself daydreaming, go back to focusing on your breathing or your word or image.

SCRIPTURE AND REFLECTION

Each sharing time will include a Scripture reading and a reflection on what the Bible says about a dimension of your marriage relationship. The reflection focuses on one particular aspect of the Scripture passage. Read the Scripture and reflection aloud. You could take turns reading to each other. You could alternate reading the Scripture and reflection.

Discuss them in the light of your relationship. Do you have a new insight? Does the reading remind you of something in your relationship that is important to discuss? Is there something from your day that you want to share that is related?

Expect that God will speak to you through the Scripture passage that you are reading and reflecting on. Come to the Scriptures with an open attitude and a sense of excitement that God's spirit will speak to you as you place yourselves under the Word. The goal here is not to understand the passage of Scripture in and of itself but to discover what this passage says to your unique relationship. Does it open a window of insight? Does it prompt questions? Does it challenge or encourage? Allow the reflection to lead you into areas of meaningful conversation.

PRAYER

The devotions provide prayers to be read aloud for each other. In addition you will want to pray personal prayers either silently or aloud. Verbal prayer may be something you are not used to. It is merely talking to God in an open and honest way. Use the language you normally use, and express whatever you wish. You may pray silently at first, but you will grow as you share verbal prayers together.

Prayer, as an area of mystery between God and us, has much about it that we do not understand and cannot explain. We do know that the Bible definitely indicates that we should pray. In fact, in the Gospels, Jesus provides much teaching on prayer. He invites us to explore the ways in which prayer can enhance our relationship with God. Throughout the letters of Paul and other New Testament writers, we find both prayers and appeals to us to pray.

In the matter of praying with others, we find some clear indications that it was normal practice in the church, and certain examples illustrate how strong an experience it was for the early church. In Acts 4:23–31 we find this description of a group of disciples gathered in prayer:

And being let go, they went to their own companions and reported all that the chief priests and elders had said to them. So when they heard that, they raised their voice to God with one accord and said: "Lord, You are God, who made heaven and earth and the sea, and all that is in them, who by the mouth of Your servant David have said:

'Why did the nations rage,
And the people plot vain things?
The kings of the earth took their stand,
And the rulers were gathered together
Against the LORD and against His Christ.'

"For truly against Your holy Servant Jesus, whom You anointed, both Herod and Pontius Pilate, with the Gentiles and the people of Israel, were gathered together to do whatever Your hand and Your purpose determined before to be done. Now, Lord, look on their threats, and grant to Your servants that with all boldness they may speak Your word, by stretching out Your hand to heal, and that signs and wonders may be done through the name of Your holy Servant Jesus." And when they had prayed, the place where they were assembled together was shaken; and they were all filled with the Holy Spirit, and they spoke the word of God with boldness.

Other references you may want to read include Luke 18:1–8; John 15:12–17; Ephesians 6:18; and Philippians 4:4–7.

Additional books on prayer are listed in the recommended reading section in the back of this book. You may want to read some of them to expand your awareness of and the use of prayer.

JOURNALING

The things you share with your partner in this devotional time may reveal an insight, a feeling, or a concern that you want to remember. Each day record what seems important to you. From time to time, you may want to return to these thoughts that you have recorded. In the years ahead the excitement, sharing, and insights of these days of marriage will provide a source of renewal.

Journaling is different from keeping a diary. It captures a significant meaning, movement, or response to what is happening. It is a recording of your inner journey as you participate in these exercises. You are charting the journey of two persons responding to God and to each other. Record things that seem vital to you in terms of joy, struggle, questions, remembrances, or continuing conversation.

Another aspect of this exercise may develop for you. You may find your personal spiritual life growing. You will be exploring the edges of your relationship with and experience of God. This will be especially true if your religion up to this point has been one of rules, rituals, and regulations. That is, if you have been thinking of a God who is only impersonal and distant, your religion may have been mostly a matter of ideas in your head. These experiences may begin to reveal to you a more personal God. You may experience feelings and sensations of a presence and awareness that are different from anything you have ever experienced before.

This new awareness is a part of what the Bible describes as an experience of the personal, active presence of God. God is personal and living and in touch with all creation, including you. As you seek to be open and receptive, God will come. The image in Revelation 3:20— "Behold, I stand at the door and knock. If anyone . . . opens the door, I will come in to him and dine with him"—describes the way in which our Lord seeks to dwell with and within us. As you receive His coming with open hospitality, you will find that presence coming into your life. Receive that presence with joy, and seek to grow in a faithful response to where it will lead you.

BLESSING

The closing part of each devotion is a blessing. We live far from the time when most people sought a blessing from someone. In fact, at one time, everyday speech was punctuated with blessings offered to one another in "hellos" and "good-byes." Blessing one another was part of the daily ritual of living together. Of course, cursing also existed. When you listen to contemporary speech, cursing is heard more often than blessing. We do have the power to curse or to bless.

The Bible describes that power in this way:

> For every kind of beast and bird, of reptile and creature of the sea, is tamed and has been tamed by mankind. But no man can tame the tongue. It is an unruly evil, full of deadly poison. With it we bless our God and Father, and with it we curse men, who have been made in the similitude of God. Out of the same mouth proceed blessing and cursing. My brethren, these things ought not to be so. Does a spring send forth fresh water and bitter from the same opening? Can a fig tree, my brethren, bear olives, or a grapevine bear figs? Thus no spring yields both salt water and fresh (James 3:7–12).

The act of blessing is grounded in the realization that God is present in everyday life and bestows grace on you. You become channels of that grace to each other through the words you share.

A blessing is more than a wish or a desire. It is more

than a prayer. It is a gift that cannot be taken away. When the gift is given in God's name, it is a gift from God to be carried within you.

You may share the blessing with each other, speaking the words firmly and graciously. Speak the words in a spirit of gift giving. When you hear them spoken to you, receive them and carry them with you. You may place your hands on your partner's head or shoulders as you speak the blessing.

THE THIRTY-DAY EXPERIMENT

I call this an experiment because it is meant to allow you to discover a way in which spiritual intimacy can grow in your relationship. Out of this experiment you will learn some things about yourselves and your relationship. You will discover ways of praying together that work and some that don't. Let your style of spiritual discipline emerge from this experiment.

A word of caution is in order. Don't think of what you are doing in these devotionals as totally spiritual and separate from other aspects of your life together. Your relationship is of one piece. There is a spiritual dimension to everything you do and are. These exercises focus on helping you discover a common journey with some particular spiritual exercises that will develop your sensitivity to the spiritual aspect of your married life.

DAY
1

The Joy Continues

SILENCE

Use this time to center yourselves and attain a measure of quietness within and without. Refer to the section in the first part of the book on silence if you are unsure about how to do this.

SCRIPTURE

On the third day there was a wedding in Cana of Galilee, and the mother of Jesus was there. Now both Jesus and His disciples were invited to the wedding. And when they ran out of wine, the mother of

Jesus said to Him, "They have no wine." Jesus said to her, "Woman, what does your concern have to do with Me? My hour has not yet come." His mother said to the servants, "Whatever He says to you, do it." Now there were set there six waterpots of stone, according to the manner of purification of the Jews, containing twenty or thirty gallons apiece. Jesus said to them, "Fill the waterpots with water." And they filled them up to the brim. And He said to them, "Draw some out now, and take it to the master of the feast." And they took it. When the master of the feast had tasted the water that was made wine, and did not know where it came from (but the servants who had drawn the water knew), the master of the feast called the bridegroom. And he said to him, "Every man at the beginning sets out the good wine, and when the guests have well drunk, then the inferior. You have kept the good wine until now!" This beginning of signs Jesus did in Cana of Galilee, and manifested His glory; and His disciples believed in Him (John 2:1–11).

ℛEFLECTION

No doubt your wedding day was an experience of joy. With your commitment made public in the midst of family and friends and in the delight of each other, it was a day full of excitement.

In the story of the wedding at Cana, Jesus' presence made a big difference in the continuing celebration. More than the presence of wine, however, was the sign or intent of His miracle. Jesus was making a statement about His presence bringing in the new wine of the kingdom of God and restoring joy to a people lost in their bondage and hopelessness. It also continues the story that where Jesus' presence is, there is the kingdom of God. To ask Jesus to bless your wedding and your marriage is to ask to have the kingdom of God present to you in your marriage.

God's presence will supply things to your marriage that you cannot give to yourselves or that other people cannot give to you. Continue to invite Jesus into your marriage, and the water of life will keep being transformed into wine—a sign of the ongoing joy in your life together.

Share the thoughts and feelings that this passage and reflection bring to mind.

$\mathscr{P}$RAYER

Gracious Lord Jesus, we are beginning a new and somewhat scary journey together. We begin it with You and pray that Your presence will be with us in all the moments we share together. Bless us with continuing joy that we may live through the days ahead in confidence and hope. Give us Your Holy Spirit that we may live and serve in love. Amen.

Share other concerns and thoughts in prayer.

$\mathscr{J}$OURNALING
Take time to record what seems important to you.

_____

_____

_____

_____

_____

_____

_____

_____

_____

_____

_____

_____

_____

_____

_____

_____

_____

ℬLESSING

*May God cause the love within you to bubble
up with joy when you think of me.*

DAY
2

The Fragrance of Love

SILENCE

Take a few moments of silence together to center yourselves. Enjoy the silence. Try to feel the freedom and pleasure that just being still in the presence of God brings to you.

SCRIPTURE

Therefore be imitators of God as dear children. And walk in love, as Christ also has loved us and given Himself for us, an offering and a sacrifice to God for a sweet-smelling aroma (Eph. 5:1–2).

ℛEFLECTION

What do you want your marriage to smell like? Do you think that's a strange question? Look at the imagery used in this Scripture to describe love: "An offering and a sacrifice to God for a sweet-smelling aroma."

For people with a discriminating sense of smell, a sweet fragrance denotes harmony and tranquillity—an at-oneness.

God has loved you with that sweet-smelling love. An aroma of oneness and harmony comes from the love that God gave to you in the self-giving act of offering up His Son, Jesus. This action of God was a sacrifice. Like a burnt offering on an altar, Christ was offered for the sake of your salvation and peace with God. When love takes on that sacrificial form, it becomes like an offering of burnt sacrifice or rare perfume.

You are called to be imitators of God by sharing this sacrificial aspect of love. When you freely give what is needed or desired to the one you love, you create a sweet-smelling environment. Oneness and harmony emerge as you are drawn to each other in that self-giving.

When you forgive each other, anticipate needs, or do a little something extra, a sweet aroma of harmony arises.

Share your thoughts and reflections that grow out of your reading of this Scripture passage and reflection.

$\mathscr{P}$RAYER

As our days of living together continue in love, O God, grant us the insight and understanding to anticipate each other's needs. Give us a strong desire to be willing to sacrifice for each other. May Your Holy Spirit strengthen us to be imitators of You so that we may live in an ongoing environment of a sweet-smelling aroma. In Jesus' name, Amen.

Share your prayer concerns.

$\mathscr{J}$OURNALING

Take time to record what seems important to you.

_____

_____

_____

_____

_____

_____

_____

_____

_____

_____

_____

_____

_____

_____

_____

_____

_____

_____

_____

_____

_____

_____

_____

_____

_____

_____

_____

*B*LESSING

*Like the soft scent of a rose carried on the
night air, may your self-giving love
delight those around you.*

DAY
3

Ecstasy in Love

SILENCE

Light a candle and share a few minutes of silence together.

SCRIPTURE

Set me as a seal upon your heart,
as a seal upon your arm;
for love is strong as death,
passion fierce as the grave.
Its flashes are flashes of fire,
a raging flame.

Many waters cannot quench love,
neither can floods drown it.
If one offered for love
all the wealth of his house
it would be utterly scorned
(Song of Sol. 8:6–7 NRSV).

$\mathcal{R}$EFLECTION

For thousands of years, poets have searched for images to describe the joy of love. There is something elusive about capturing the mystery of how two people are drawn together and find great delight in each other. Ecstasy is one of love's most profound characteristics.

Notice the images in this passage: "Love is strong as death . . . passion fierce as the grave . . . a raging flame."

The decision to marry is like an invitation: "Come away with me, my beloved." You are invited to come from being alone into the joy of being together with the beloved. The thought of a relationship of love prompts the response to the age-old description: "A man shall leave his father and mother and be joined to his wife, and they shall become one flesh" (Gen. 2:24).

The depth of joy described here in the Song of Solomon is deeper than a superficial response to beauty. You desire to share life together—not just a few fleeting moments. You realize that with the beloved you can find a lasting ecstasy.

Some marriages grow cold and flat—they need not. Ecstasy can grow as time spent together lengthens. Appreciation of the mystery and beauty of each other can grow through the years. Reveal yourselves and delight in each other.

Share your reflections on this passage.

*P*RAYER

Lord Jesus, we invite Your presence into our life together. Bring your love to touch what we feel for each other so that our love may be deepened. Draw us into Your presence so that our joy may be full. Remove the barriers to joy so that we may experience an ever-expanding sense of Your love. Lord, we thank You for giving us eyes to see the beauty of each other. In Your name, Amen.

Share your personal prayer thoughts.

*J*OURNALING

Take time to record what seems important to you.

_____

_____

_____

_____

_____

_____

_____

_____

_____

_____

_____

_____

_____

_____

_____

_____

_____

_____

_____

_____

ℬLESSING

*May God fan the fire of our love with a
continuous breath of delight in each other.*

DAY
4

Two Become One

SILENCE

For a few minutes, let the cares of the day be put aside, and seek to be still, relaxed, and quiet together. Allow an image of God's peaceful presence to be the focus of your thoughts.

SCRIPTURE

Therefore a man shall leave his father and mother and be joined to his wife, and they shall become one flesh (Gen. 2:24).

ℛEFLECTION

Do you ever sense how different you are from each other? Each of you has a unique history and personality. You have been developing as a person and are being created within yourself, but now you are joined to another and called into an experience of oneness.

Understanding this oneness will be part of your journey together in marriage. You will find yourselves called to experience this oneness in various ways, and each way will open an area for exploration into this new territory.

This journey toward oneness does not mean that both partners become alike. Each can remain an individual. It does mean being open to receiving all that the other person is and being willing to share who you are.

Think of this process as unlayering your life and gradually revealing who you are. Through the days, months, and years ahead, both will slowly come to experience more oneness. The strength of that unity will be found in the capacity to receive each other's differences and allow them to complement and enrich each other.

Whether in lovemaking, conversation, prayer, or work together, each opportunity to reveal and accept the other will deepen the experience of oneness. Your relationship becomes the primary connection; others such as parents, family, and friends become secondary.

For some, this task of marriage is easy. For others, it is hard. From time to time, examine your priorities on your journey to oneness.

Share your reflections on oneness.

*P*RAYER

O God, be the light on our path to oneness. Continually open our eyes to see the way to move toward sharing and being together that we may be all we can be, alone and together.

Pray your thoughts together.

*J*OURNALING

Take time to record what seems important to you.

_____

_____

_____

_____

_____

_____

_____

_____

_____

_____

_____

_____

_____

_____

_____

_____

_____

_____

_____

_____

_____

_____

_____

_____

_____

_____

ℬLESSING

*May the loneliness within when we are absent
from each other be overcome with contentment
when we are together.*

DAY
5

The Endurance of Love

SILENCE

Continue to seek stillness, silence, and solitude. Stretch the silence a little beyond the time you feel like quitting.

SCRIPTURE

Love is patient; love is kind; love is not envious or boastful or arrogant or rude. It does not insist on its own way; it is not irritable or resentful; it does not rejoice in wrongdoing, but rejoices in the truth. It bears all things, believes all things, hopes all things, endures all things (1 Cor. 13:4–7 NRSV).

$\mathcal{R}$EFLECTION

It is exciting to see the way God draws people together through chemistry. Love manifests itself in a strong
desire to be together because it is exciting. This attraction
is important to bring two people together to begin a relationship. Attraction may be appearance, attitudes, ideas,
or temperament. This original attraction may or may not
endure.

However, by binding yourselves together with wedding vows, you have said that the union is going to last.
Will the excitement always be there? Will the ecstasy
always remain? It may fade for a time. What happens then?
Does it mean that love is lost?

By no means. The dimension of love that will give
your marriage its enduring quality will be the commitment you have made. This commitment to love, despite
feelings that may or may not be there, is the love described
in 1 Corinthians 13. A gracious gift from God has made
you want to bind yourself to this other person. Ecstasy is
the love that is prompted by your delight in each other.
Agape love comes from within you to care for and to
commit to the other even when he or she is not creating
joy or good feelings in you.

This agape love is connected to your will and desire to
love in spite of misunderstandings, miscommunications,
or hurts. Agape love creates the motivation to remain
bonded no matter what happens to pull you apart.

Is this love possible? Many have found it. It comes not
only from you but as a gift from God—freely and beauti-
fully offered as your heart and will open to God.

Share your thoughts on this aspect of your love for each other.

$\mathcal{P}$RAYER

*Heavenly Father, we thank You for the eternal commitment
You have made to us. In Jesus, You have sealed us for life and
eternity. We thank You for the commitment You have made to
be with us and in us for the time we share together in this life.
Give to us such a clear commitment to each other that we
will be sustained in the power of Your love. Give to us,
O God, the love that endures. Amen.*

Take a few moments for personal silent prayer asking
God to fill you with a sense of agape love.

$\mathcal{J}$OURNALING

Take time to record what seems important to you.

_____

_____

_____

_____

_____

_____

_____

_____

_____

_____

_____

_____

_____

_____

_____

_____

_____

_____

_____

_____

_____

_____

_____

$\mathscr{B}$LESSING

*May God's steadfast love dwell in the deepest
places of your heart to give you strength to
understand and forgive.*

DAY
6

Tender-hearted Love

SILENCE

Take time to share some moments of silence together. Use your image or word to concentrate if you are distracted from seeking stillness.

SCRIPTURE

Let all bitterness, wrath, anger, clamor, and evil speaking be put away from you, with all malice. And be kind to one another, tenderhearted, forgiving one another, even as God in Christ forgave you (Eph. 4:31–32).

ℛEFLECTION

Difficulties face a man and a woman who come together in marriage. You will not always see eye to eye. You will not always understand each other's behavior. You will hurt each other by things you say or don't say. Sometimes you will be insensitive to the other person. It happens.

This Scripture speaks about being tenderhearted and forgiving each other. From where does a tender heart come?

The clue lies in the last part: "As God in Christ forgave you." If you live with a lively sense of being accepted and forgiven by God for all your mistakes and failures, you have a cleansed feeling and a soft heart. Hearts are softened by honest confession and by the forgiveness of another.

Your relationship will be deepened and strengthened to the degree that you can live with a rhythm of confession and forgiveness. That means moving beyond a defensive posture that is afraid to admit to a mistake or failure.

An unwillingness to be honest about your weaknesses or failures will create a hardness of heart. The Bible uses this phrase to describe an unwillingness to change and bend to a path of reconciliation with God or another.

The alternative to this hard heart is a tender heart. A heart willing to be open about hurts or insensitivities will experience this softness and will enter into a forgiving and forgiven stance.

That will not always be easy. In certain areas of your life you can be extremely defensive and unwilling to admit a problem. Accepting what your partner is saying about a certain behavior that is causing hurt will make you feel weak and defenseless.

At times like that, try to overcome your defensiveness and be willing to change by admitting to yourself that that is true and you are sorry for what you have done. You will open the door to forgiveness and create a tender heart toward each other.

Share your reflections in response to the phrase about being tenderhearted.

RAYER

Gracious Lord, we thank You for the gift of forgiveness. Break us open to tenderness in those places in our lives where we have allowed a hardness of heart to develop. Strengthen our sense of being forgiven by You, O Lord, so that we may be given the strength to admit those areas of our lives where we need to forgive each other. In Jesus' name, Amen.

Share your prayers focusing on seeking a tender heart.

OURNALING

Take time to record what seems important to you.

_____

_____

_____

_____

_____

_____

_____

_____

_____

_____

_____

_____

_____

_____

_____

_____

_____

_____

_____

_____

_____

_____

ℬLESSING

*God bless you with tenderness that you may
enjoy all the gifts that come to you.*

DAY
7

Friendship

$\int$ILENCE

Share a quiet and still time together. Don't rush by this quiet time. Seek a very still presence and let yourself focus on being open to the presence of God. This month, as the days go by, let your quiet time lengthen.

$\int$CRIPTURE

This is my commandment, that you love one another as I have loved you. No one has greater love than this, to lay down one's life for one's friends. You are my friends if you do what I command you. I do not

call you servants any longer, because the servant
does not know what the master is doing; but I have
called you friends, because I have made known to
you everything that I have heard from my Father.
You did not choose me, but I chose you. And I ap-
pointed you to go and bear fruit, fruit that will last,
so that the Father will give you whatever you ask
him in my name. I am giving you these commands
so that you may love one another (John 15:12–17
NRSV).

$\mathscr{R}$EFLECTION

When people tell you what they think friendship is,
they usually say something about trusting, being willing
to share what is inside, or accepting them with their faults.
These comments touch on the most important part of
friendship, and friendship is a fundamental part of marriage.

Some people jokingly talk about remaining friends instead of getting married. This dichotomy between friendship and marriage ought not to exist. I hope that
friendship is something you brought with you into your
marriage and will be something that will grow with your
marriage.

In the Scripture above, Jesus talks about the nature of
His friendship with His disciples. He describes that
friendship as one in which He has not withheld Himself
or what He knows from them. He has tried to create an
equality between them by sharing with them.

By not withholding but by sharing your knowledge
and gifts, you will find your friendship growing, which

creates enjoyment in being together. As you share your wants, needs, ideas, opinions, and feelings, you will find common ground out of which to live.

The essence of friendship is enjoying being together and being comfortable and supportive no matter what you are doing. This aspect of marriage needs recurring renewal. Ongoing open communication keeps alive the sense of growing together and establishes and reestablishes a common basis for being together.

Share with each other the meaning of your friendship within your marriage.

$\mathscr{P}$RAYER

Holy Spirit, You move in us and between us. We thank You for the experience of friendship You have created by Your presence in our lives. Continue to undergird the love commitment with enjoyment and understanding of each other. Help us in our emotional growth so that we may be healthy companions on our way and continue to want to be with each other. Amen.

Share your prayer thoughts.

$\mathscr{J}$OURNALING
Take time to record what seems important to you.

_____

_____

_____

_____

_____

_____

_____

_____

_____

_____

_____

_____

_____

_____

_____

_____

_____

_____

$\mathcal{B}$LESSING

*May God bless you through the bonds of our
friendship with which I tie myself to you.*

DAY
8

Share
Your
Gifts

SILENCE

Find your comfortable posture. Breathe naturally. Let yourself relax throughout your whole body. Seek that still and quiet inner place, letting all your thoughts and concerns pass through your mind. Use your word or image to focus.

SCRIPTURE

Now concerning spiritual gifts, brothers and sisters, I do not want you to be uninformed. You know that when you were pagans, you were enticed and led astray to idols that could not speak. Therefore I want you to understand that no one speaking by the Spirit of God ever says "Let Jesus be cursed!" and no one can say "Jesus is Lord" except by the Holy Spirit.

Now there are varieties of gifts, but the same Spirit; and there are varieties of services, but the same Lord; and there are varieties of activities, but it is the same God who activates all of them in everyone. To each is given the manifestation of the Spirit for the common good. To one is given through the Spirit the utterance of wisdom, and to another the utterance of knowledge according to the same Spirit, to another faith by the same Spirit, to another gifts of healing by the one Spirit, to another the working of miracles, to another prophecy, to another the discernment of spirits, to another various kinds of tongues, to another the interpretation of tongues. All these are activated by one and the same Spirit, who allots to each one individually just as the Spirit chooses (1 Cor. 12:1–11 NRSV).

$\mathscr{R}$EFLECTION

God gives gifts to the Christian community so that its members may be enabled to serve one another and the world. In the midst of your community in marriage, God will manifest spiritual gifts through each of you. God works in this wonderful way among people. Who you are and what you have are not meant for you alone. You are meant to be a channel of care, strength, and hope to others. You are God's grace-filled gift to your partner.

What you can give to each other is not just what you

bring to your relationship as a person. God supplies the spiritual gifts you need for your marriage to work and to be a blessing to you and others. God will work through you in unique ways.

God gives gifts, as the Scriptures clearly show. Pray for the gifts needed for your relationship to grow and prosper. Expect God to manifest the Spirit to meet your needs. Trust in God's desire to bless and provide for you. Act on the prompting of God's spirit to pray for your partner and to share the words and gifts God gives you.

Discuss the gifts you bring to each other. Is your partner aware of a gift you have that you do not know about?

RAYER

O God, help us to remember that we do not own each other.
We belong to You, and You have gifted us with each other. In
that spirit let us offer ourselves to each other, trusting that each
will be received as a gift and not possessed as a thing owned.
Continue to reveal Your love to us that we may freely
offer and receive love from each other. Amen.

Add your own prayers.

OURNALING
Take time to record what seems important to you.

_____

_____

_____

_____

_____

_____

_____

_____

_____

_____

_____

_____

_____

_____

_____

_____

_____

_____

$\mathscr{B}$LESSING

*May God's love encourage and guide the
Spirit's gifts in your life.*

DAY
9

The Unseen Guest

$\mathcal{S}$ILENCE

Continue your practice of silence for beginning these shared devotions. Remember that you are trying to detach yourself from the world around you and the world within so that you may be still and receptive to the presence of God. Each time let the silence be extended a little beyond when you want to quit.

$\mathcal{S}$CRIPTURE

When the Son of Man comes in His glory, and all the holy angels with Him, then He will sit on the throne of His glory. All the nations will be gathered before Him, and He will separate them one from another, as a shepherd divides his sheep from the goats. And He will set the sheep on His right hand, but the goats on the left. Then the King will say to those on His right hand, "Come, you blessed of My Father, inherit the kingdom prepared for you from the foundation of the world: for I was hungry and you gave Me food; I was thirsty and you gave Me drink; I was a stranger and you took Me in; I was naked and you clothed Me; I was sick and you visited Me; I was in prison and you came to Me." Then the righteous will answer Him, saying, "Lord, when did we see You hungry and feed You, or thirsty and give You drink? When did we see You a stranger and take You in, or naked and clothe You? Or when did we see You sick, or in prison, and come to You?" And the King will answer and say to them, "Assuredly, I say to you, inasmuch as you did it to one of the least of these My brethren, you did it to Me" (Matt. 25:31–40).

ℛEFLECTION

Permitting Jesus to enter your relationship and shape your marriage will mean discovering new edges to your life together. Jesus always seems to bring others when He comes. He is never separate from those to whom He expresses much love and compassion. The story from Matthew describes the way in which Jesus identified Himself with the poor, sick, and suffering.

As you continue with these meditations, you may find yourself being drawn toward thoughts of charity and caring toward others. It is a natural outgrowth of sharing your life with Christ. He begins to show you how to share with others.

In this way Christ will open up another aspect of vocation for your marriage. Together you may discover that you have time, gifts, and concerns that will help and care for others.

Marriage has a social dimension. Your community of two is related to other larger communities to which you belong. Your families are included in this as well as other social relationships. In the earliest days of your marriage you may want to concentrate primarily on each other. That is important and necessary, but gradually, you will open up your lives to others who really need you.

Examine your gifts in the light of others' needs that seem to call out to you. As time goes on, let them become an occasion for conversation. You will find yourselves being drawn into the larger community because that is where you will find Christ. This sharing will also do wonders for your marriage.

Talk about how you respond to this parable of Jesus and this reflection.

$\mathscr{P}$RAYER

Gracious God, You have chosen to love and care for the poor of the earth. Help us to find ways to include them in our lives. Enlarge the circle of our awareness that we may begin to experience Your hidden presence through seeing those who are in need. Help us not to close off our love and concern for ones who need our assistance. Keep us on the humble path. Amen.

Share your prayer thoughts for persons you feel need your love and support.

$\mathscr{J}$OURNALING

Take time to record what seems important to you.

$\mathscr{B}$LESSING

*God bless you with wisdom to recognize
the Lord's presence in others.*

DAY
10

Take Time to Listen

SILENCE

Remember that you are seeking to be hospitable to God and to your partner during this time of silence. Let all other things pass from your mind, and prepare an open heart to receive them. Let your breathing be natural and flowing. Imagine the spirit of God entering you as you inhale. Focus on God's presence.

SCRIPTURE

Now it happened as they went that He entered a certain village; and a certain woman named Martha welcomed Him into her house. And she had a sister called Mary, who also sat at Jesus' feet and heard His word. But Martha was distracted with much serving, and she approached Him and said, "Lord, do You not care that my sister has left me to serve alone? Therefore tell her to help me."

And Jesus answered and said to her, "Martha, Martha, you are worried and troubled about many things. But one thing is needed, and Mary has chosen that good part, which will not be taken away from her" (Luke 10:38–42).

ℛEFLECTION

Can you visualize this scene clearly? There are two different responses to Jesus' presence. Martha expresses her sense of hospitality by providing food and an environment that will allow Jesus to relax and feel at home. Mary puts herself at the feet of Jesus, focusing on Him as a person and concentrating on what He is saying. Both are hospitable acts. However, Martha becomes irritated with Mary and seems to think that her hospitality should take priority. At this point Jesus defends Mary's hospitality and affirms focusing on His presence and receiving Him inwardly.

In your life together these two aspects of hospitality for each other are important. Be attentive to the outward form of hospitality for each other, but do not neglect inward hospitality.

There are times to listen carefully to each other. The things you do for each other are significant, but how you pay attention and receive each other inwardly is the better part.

Share your reflections on your hospitality toward each other. Is your listening capacity growing? Is your sensitivity to your partner's mood expanding?

*P*RAYER

O God, we thank You for the gift of ears enabling us to hear and listen to each other. We thank You also for the gift of a heart to use those ears to be open and attentive to each other. Remind us often, O God, to be hospitable to each other, sitting at each other's feet and receiving the other's thoughts, dreams, and concerns. Help us not only to do for each other but to be for each other. We pray in Your gracious name, Amen.

Share your personal prayers.

*J*OURNALING
Take time to record what seems important to you.

_____

_____

_____

_____

_____

_____

_____

_____

$\mathcal{B}$LESSING

*May God be your inner ear to listen
with balance and wisdom.*

DAY
11

*Share
in Weakness*

SILENCE

These silent times may bring you a sense of vulnerability and weakness. Don't be anxious about it. Your weakness will become a source of trust and hope. As you share this silence, let the sense of weakness be an occasion for you to realize that you are dependent on God and this other person. In your weakness you are loved and accepted.

SCRIPTURE

Jesus answered them, saying, "The hour has come that the Son of Man should be glorified. Most assuredly, I say to you, unless a grain of wheat falls into the ground and dies, it remains alone; but if it dies, it produces much grain. He who loves his life will lose it, and he who hates his life in this world will keep it for eternal life. If anyone serves Me, let him follow Me; and where I am, there My servant will be also. If anyone serves Me, him My Father will honor" (John 12:23–26).

ℛEFLECTION

In this Scripture, Jesus describes His own attitude and behavior in giving His life for the sake of the kingdom. He describes an attitude that is hard for us to grasp.

You may feel life is something to hold on to. You may find it hard to let go and allow someone else to determine your life. And yet, if your life is to produce the proper fruit, it needs to die so that something new can be born. As you share your life in expressions of love, following Jesus' lead, that love will produce more life in others. Following Jesus is a call to be a life giver by sharing yourself with others. Then your life will be filled with God's love and purpose.

Too often strength is interpreted as the capacity to hold on to who you are and to what you have. You imagine that your life is strong when you retain control and focus on getting for yourself rather than giving away to others. This position is dangerous. It can easily turn into selfishness and self-serving.

To die to self is to release life for others by giving your life to them. It may appear as weakness, but in the end it is true strength.

Discuss your thoughts about this reflection.

RAYER

O God, help us to see the way of death that frees us to share in life for ourselves and for others. Help us to let go and not seek to possess ourselves so strongly that we are not used for others in a life-giving way. Show us the way of strength revealed in Jesus that frees us to die so that we may truly live. Save us from the weakness that lives in fear so that we may let go and let God. Amen.

Share your prayers together.

OURNALING

Take time to record what seems important to you.

_____

_____

_____

_____

_____

_____

_____

_____

_____

43

_____

_____

_____

_____

_____

_____

_____

_____

_____

_____

_____

_____

_____

_____

_____

ℬLESSING

*May you always know God's strength
present in your weakness.*

DAY
12

*Receive
and Reflect
Love*

$\mathcal{S}$ILENCE

In your silence you are seeking the presence of God who loves you. God is present. Release your concerns and enter your silence with a desire to know the loving presence that God gives you.

$\mathcal{S}$CRIPTURE

Beloved, let us love one another, for love is of God; and everyone who loves is born of God and knows God. He who does not love does not know God, for

God is love. In this the love of God was manifested toward us, that God has sent His only begotten Son into the world, that we might live through Him. In this is love, not that we loved God, but that He loved us and sent His Son to be the propitiation for our sins. Beloved, if God so loved us, we also ought to love one another (1 John 4:7–11).

$\mathscr{R}$EFLECTION

You love because God has loved you. But you know you love God because you love each other. In this Bible passage love for each other becomes a test of whether or not you love God.

That may sound like double-talk, but a great truth is being communicated. God's self-giving love has come from beyond you in the person of Jesus who gave His life for you. This manifestation of God's love demonstrates to you how deep and unconditional that love is. By the cross of Christ, you know God's love for you. You reflect that love back to God by loving each other in the same self-giving way. You and others know that you have received God's love if you love each other.

Does your love for each other have anything to do with your relationship with God? This passage would seem to say that it does. In fact, if your love is to reach depths of love connected to unconditional acceptance and sacrificial self-giving to each other, it does have something to do with God. This kind of love is a gift from God and grows out of the experience of having been loved like that.

A young couple discovered that both were raised in families that expressed love only by yelling at and hitting each other. Neither was capable of giving expression to love through caring, forgiveness, or acceptance. When that sort of love was called for in their relationship, they would swing at each other.

They had not been nurtured on the love God has demonstrated in Jesus. They were confused by their behavior. They knew something was wrong, but they couldn't figure it out because that dimension of unconditional acceptance and forgiveness was not in their experience as a way of receiving and reflecting love.

God belongs in your relationship if your love is to reach its fullest and deepest expression.

Share your thoughts on this Scripture and reflection.

$\mathscr{P}$RAYER

O God, You have loved us in a most deep and profound way. Strengthen our trust in You so that it becomes a channel through which Your love can flow to us and between us. Without the gift of Your unconditional and sacrificial love, we struggle to be fully loving in our relationship. Fill the silent moments we share with a sense of Your loving presence in and between us. Amen.

Spend some silent moments seeking to be still. Focus on receiving a gift of God's love that can be shared with your partner.

$\mathscr{J}$OURNALING

Take time to record what seems important to you.

_____

_____

_____

_____

_____

_____

_____

_____

_____

_____

_____

_____

_____

$\mathscr{B}$LESSING

*May your every deed shine with love from
God reflected from the mirror of your heart.*

DAY
13

Obedience and Love

SILENCE

Seek a calm, centered place within yourself. Do not be anxious to have the time pass quickly. Savor the stillness.

SCRIPTURE

Be subject to one another out of reverence for Christ. Wives, be subject to your husbands as you are to the Lord. For the husband is the head of the wife just as Christ is the head of the church, the body of which he is the Savior. Just as the church is subject to Christ, so also wives ought to be, in everything, to their husbands. Husbands, love your wives, just as Christ loved the church and gave himself up for her, in order to make her holy by cleansing her with the washing of water by the word, so as to present the church to himself in splendor, without a spot or wrinkle or anything of the kind—yes, so that she may be holy and without blemish. In the same way, husbands should love their wives as they do their own bodies. He who loves his wife loves himself (Eph. 5:21–28 NRSV).

$\mathscr{R}$EFLECTION

Obedience, especially as it has been described in this passage of Scripture, generates some hot discussion between men and women. Because of the imbalance between men and women in relation to authority and power, obedience carries for some a meaning very close to that of slavery.

The key verse is the first verse quoted: "Be subject to one another out of reverence for Christ." This verse describes a mutual obedience to each other. To be subject to each other is to be guided in action and thought by the needs and person of the other. There are mutual respect, love, and serving of the other. This mutual obedience is called for out of reverence for Christ. That is, each is to see the other as being in Christ.

The apostle Paul then goes on to state specifically how this applies to men and women. He defines it in terms of obedience for women and self-sacrificing love for men. With the changing role of men and women in society, family, and church, we would use different language to talk about the application of the basic principle in this Scripture. However, the basic thought remains an important teaching in understanding the life women and men are called to live together in marriage. Be obedient, and give yourself in love to each other out of reverence for Christ.

How do you understand obedience to each other? How do you give yourself up to sacrificial love for your partner? Is seeing Christ in your partner a way to help the discussion define obedience for you?

$\mathscr{P}$RAYER

Our Savior and Lord, let our love for each other bring forth a mutual obedience that will bring joy and strength to our marriage. Don't let us be tyrants. Deliver us from disrespect for each other. Let Your love be the filter through which our actions flow so that we may be built up in every way through the life we are living together. In Your name we pray, Amen.

Share your prayer concerns from the day.

$\mathscr{J}$OURNALING

Take time to record what seems important to you.

_____

_____

_____

_____

_____

_____

_____

_____

_____

_____

_____

_____

_____

_____

_____

_____

_____

_____

$\mathscr{B}$LESSING

*God bless you with a walk on the path of
obedience lit by your love for me.*

DAY
14

Bearing
and
Forbearing

SILENCE

Stay with your silence until you feel relaxed and centered within yourself. Review the section on silence in the first part of the book if you are having problems with it.

SCRIPTURE

My friends, if anyone is detected in a transgression, you who have received the Spirit should restore such a one in a spirit of gentleness. Take care that you yourselves are not tempted. Bear one another's burdens, and in this way you will fulfill the law of Christ (Gal. 6:1–2 NRSV).

ℛEFLECTION

How easily people jump on others when they do wrong, make a mistake, or act in a sinful way. Usually, people tend to add to their burden of guilt by passing judgment on them and calling attention to what they have done. The apostle Paul encourages an attitude of forbearance, that is, withholding judgment and maintaining a relationship of acceptance with the person. This is good advice in a marriage.

There are so many opportunities in marriage to offend the other because you are so closely entwined in your lives. Forbearance will allow you to continue to be together in an accepting manner without adding a larger burden of guilt on the other.

In fact, the apostle goes on to say that you are to bear each other's burdens to fulfill Christ's law of love. So you are not only to forbear but actually to bear with each other, that is, to help carry the burden of what one feels. That is what it truly means to be a partner. Just as you are partners in living a life together, so you are partners in being sinners together. At this point neither of you is better than the other. Each of you carries the stigma of sin. Instead of adding to the burden by claiming to be better or putting down the other person, help each other.

As your sharing deepens in your relationship, let your forbearance deepen as well. More and more of the burdens each of you bears deep within will begin to come out. Help each other reveal burdens by always receiving what is shared in a spirit of compassion and support.

Share your thoughts on this Scripture and reflection.

$\mathscr{P}$RAYER

O Christ, You are the bearer of the burdens of the world including our own. Teach us by Your compassionate example to be patient with each other and forbearing toward each other. Overcome our competition with Your gift of compassion. In Jesus' name, Amen.

Add your prayer requests.

$\mathscr{J}$OURNALING

Take time to record what seems important to you.

_____

_____

_____

_____

_____

_____

_____

_____

_____

_____

_____

_____

_____

_____

_____

_____

_____

_____

_____

_____

_____

_____

_____

_____

_____

_____

_____

$\mathcal{B}$LESSING

*May the Lord's compassion be the source and
strength of your relationships.*

DAY
15

Include God

$\mathcal{S}$ILENCE

Today, light a candle during your devotion. Let it be a symbol of the presence of God. In your silent time release your hold on your house, security, and possessions. During these moments, let God take complete care of them.

$\mathcal{S}$CRIPTURE

Unless the LORD builds the house,
They labor in vain who build it;
Unless the LORD guards the city,
The watchman stays awake in vain.

It is vain for you to rise up early,
To sit up late,
To eat the bread of sorrows;
For so He gives His beloved sleep.

Behold, children are a heritage from the LORD,
The fruit of the womb is a reward.
Like arrows in the hand of a warrior,
So are the children of one's youth.
Happy is the man who has his quiver full of them;
They shall not be ashamed,
But shall speak with their enemies in the gate (Ps. 127).

ℛEFLECTION

Where is your ultimate security? You may be tempted to think of your own strength or resources. In this psalm the writer points to an important truth. The ultimate security and guarantee of a house being built or a city being protected are in God.

Think of this point in relationship to the house or household you are building. If it is to last and be what it can be, God must be involved at the level of foundation and direction.

The number of divorces today makes you wonder what is going wrong. Obviously, those who got married did not intend to divorce when they said their vows.

The absence of God as the chief architect and builder of the relationship is part of the reason for a marriage breakdown. God builds from the inside out, that is, God works in and on the people involved.

It is not the things you purchase and surround yourselves with that will make or break your marriage. It is what is going on inside each of you and, ultimately, between you in your relationship that God will use to give strength and endurance to your commitment.

The more you are able to let God build your house (your marriage) from within, the more strength and foundation it will have. Then when you lose things or struggle with difficult financial situations, your marriage will not be torn apart. Your foundation will be secure, and you will be able to rebuild the other things upon it.

Discuss what you feel are the foundation stones of your marriage.

*P*RAYER

O God, You have established the foundations of the world and brought forth a beautiful creation in which to live. Help us to discover and receive the foundation stones of faith, love, and hope in You so that our life together will have the strength to endure. Keep us from being seduced by the things of this world, good as they are, so that we do not give up the Rock of our foundation, even Jesus Christ, our Lord. Amen.

Add your prayers for the day.

*J*OURNALING

Take time to record what seems important to you.

_____

_____

_____

_____

_____

_____

_____

_____

_____

_____

_____

_____

_____

_____

_____

_____

ℬLESSING

*May you continue to discover that letting God
in never makes your life overcrowded.*

DAY
16

Be Content with Today

SILENCE

As you enter your silence today, seek to be in the moment. Let yesterday and tomorrow fade away. Sense how real the present moment can be as you seek God alone in this time. Let all anxieties move behind you.

SCRIPTURE

Therefore I tell you, do not worry about your life, what you will eat or what you will drink, or about your body, what you will wear. Is not life more than food, and the body more than clothing? Look at the birds of the air; they neither sow nor reap nor gather into barns, and yet your heavenly Father feeds them. Are you not of more value than they? And can any of you by worrying add a single hour to your span of life? And why do you worry about clothing? Consider the lilies of the field, how they grow; they neither toil nor spin; yet I tell you, even Solomon in all his glory was not clothed like one of these. But if God so clothes the grass of the field, which is alive today and tomorrow is thrown into the oven, will he not much more clothe you—you of little faith? Therefore do not worry, saying, "What will we eat?" or "What will we drink?" or "What will we wear?" For it is the Gentiles who strive for all these things; and indeed your heavenly Father knows that you need all these things. But strive first for the kingdom of God and his righteousness, and all these things will be given to you as well. So do not worry about tomorrow, for tomorrow will bring worries of its own. Today's trouble is enough for today (Matt. 6:25–34 NRSV).

ℛEFLECTION

It is amazing how many yesterdays and tomorrows can clutter up your life. Regrets of the past and worries about tomorrow can multiply endlessly. Life can easily become a bundle of anxieties that become heavy burdens you carry throughout each day.

Jesus encourages you to let go of these anxieties. Yesterday cannot be changed, though it can be forgiven. Tomorrow will not be affected by your anxiety. Today is the reality in which you live. Live that reality trusting in God for the past and the future.

At this point you can help each other remember this truth. From time to time, each of you may be caught in this trap. You can remind each other to let go of the anxiety of the past or the future. Call each other into the present. Worry will not change any circumstance. Some things can be changed, and other things will not change. Work on the changeable things, and learn to accept what you cannot change.

𝒫RAYER

Lord of all time, we thank You for being in all the moments of our lives. You were in our past with Your loving presence, forgiving and healing all moments. Help us give up any regrets or shame over what has gone by. You are in our future and will be present with Your guidance and sustaining strength for us. Help us give up our anxiety to You and Your promises. Lord, help us sense Your presence in each moment and drink in with confidence the blessings of that presence for our lives. In Your comforting name we pray, Amen.

Add your own prayers, especially concerns that create anxiety or fear for you.

𝒥OURNALING

Take time to record what seems important to you.

_____

_____

_____

_____

_____

_____

_____

_____

_____

_____

_____

_____

_____

_____

_____

_____

_____

_____

_____

ℬLESSING

*God give you a calm spirit like the sparrow,
which knows all things will be supplied.*

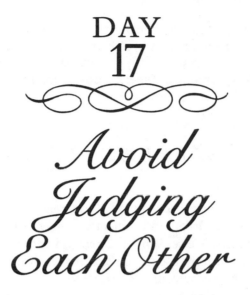

DAY
17

Avoid Judging Each Other

$\mathcal{S}$ILENCE

Relax and let your inner journey proceed to stillness and solitude. Extend your time in silence together.

$\mathcal{S}$CRIPTURE

Judge not, that you be not judged. For with what judgment you judge, you will be judged; and with the measure you use, it will be measured back to you. And why do you look at the speck in your brother's eye, but do not consider the plank in your own eye? Or how can you say to your brother, "Let me remove the speck from your eye"; and look, a plank is in your own eye? Hypocrite! First remove the plank from your own eye, and then you will see clearly to remove the speck from your brother's eye (Matt. 7:1–5).

$\mathcal{R}$EFLECTION

It is amazing how quickly you may find yourself judging others. In only a moment you may be judgmental toward someone else. What the person is doing or saying may trigger a response in you that makes you lash out at or judge the behavior in a negative way.

Jesus describes such situations in much the same way as modern psychologists talk about projections. That is, you tend to see in others the faults that are strong in you but often not acknowledged. What appears as a speck in another's eye is really a plank in your eye. To see clearly, you need to remove the plank from your eye.

When you feel judgmental toward your partner, look within yourself to see if the problem is within you. In this way you can begin to understand some of the areas in your life where you need to grow and seek transformation.

This area in the marriage relationship is difficult to deal with because it often involves looking at yourself where you have hidden away your faults. As time goes on, these judgmental attitudes can work negatively in your relationship. You may react defensively in this area. But if you proceed slowly and graciously to become aware of times when either partner becomes judgmental, you will be able to help each other accept these things in yourselves and, eventually, in each other.

Share your thoughts on this Scripture and reflection.

$\mathscr{P}$RAYER

O God, we thank You for bringing us together in love. Instill in us a great respect for each other. Keep us from judging each other so that we do not find ourselves being separated rather than being unified. Enable us to share feelings without blaming the other, and keep us from defensiveness. Help us discern our areas of growth and seek such change as we are able. Keep us on the path toward unity in You, O Lord. Amen.

Add your own prayers.

$\mathscr{J}$OURNALING
Take time to record what seems important to you.

_____

_____

_____

_____

_____

_____

_____

_____

_____

_____

_____

_____

_____

_____

_____

_____

_____

_____

_____

_____

_____

_____

_____

ℬLESSING

May God always give you the desire to
understand before the desire to judge.

DAY
18

*Can
You See
the Goodness?*

SILENCE

Share your time of silence together. As you enter the silence, let all negative thoughts and feelings pass away. Focus on sensing the goodness of God for your life. Desire a feeling of that goodness within yourself.

SCRIPTURE

It is good to give thanks to the LORD,
And to sing praises to Your name, O Most High;
To declare Your lovingkindness in the morning,
And Your faithfulness every night,

On an instrument of ten strings,
On the lute,
And on the harp,
With harmonious sound.
For You, LORD, have made me glad through
    Your work;
I will triumph in the works of Your hands
    (Ps. 92:1–4).

ℛEFLECTION

The more you get to know God, the more joy becomes a mark of your life. The theologian Teilhard Chardin said, "Joy is the infallible sign of God's presence." God's presence brings joy because God is good, that is, goodness toward His creation flows from God.

You are the object of God's goodness. Surrounding you are truly amazing gifts—gifts that are freely given and endless. God's love is there. The sky, trees, flowers, and creatures of all kinds are around you. You have the gift of each other. All of these things flow from the goodness of God. That is the way the psalm writer saw it, and he exploded in a song of praise.

Keeping your eyes focused on the goodness of God will bring celebration and joy. In the midst of all that can go wrong and upset you, God is present with goodness in many ways—not as an escape from your problems and decisions that need to be made but as a reminder to keep balance in your life and relationship. God's goodness is always present, even in the midst of darkness, confusion, or pain.

An old gospel song carries a reminder of how to focus on this goodness so that balance can be restored:

Turn your eyes upon Jesus,
Look full in His wonderful face;
And the things of earth will grow strangely dim
In the light of His glory and grace.

Share with each other signs of God's goodness that
you have seen today.

PRAYER

Gracious God, You give joy to the whole earth through Your
goodness. Let that joy be in us as Your Holy Spirit brings the
constant reminder of Your goodness that surrounds our life
together. Open our eyes to the ongoing mercies and gifts You
supply so that our lives can be sustained from day to day. Guide
us to the balance that sees Your goodness in all circumstances
in life. Through Christ, our Lord, Amen.

Share a prayer of thanks for specific gifts God has
given both of you.

JOURNALING

Take time to record what seems important to you.

_____

_____

_____

_____

_____

_____

_____

_____

_____

_____

_____

_____

_____

_____

$\mathcal{B}$LESSING

*With eyes wide open, receive the good
gifts God gives through my love
commitment to you.*

DAY
19

Pray for Each Other

SILENCE

As you share the silence today, be aware of the needs of your partner. Can you focus on some specific things for which you could pray for your partner?

SCRIPTURE

Beloved, pray for us (1 Thess. 5:25 NRSV).

ℛEFLECTION

This short verse says much. It is a request; someone is reaching and asking. And it is speaking in intimate terms when it says, "Beloved." The request is prayer. Out of the intimacy of the Christian community, the apostle Paul is making an appeal to the others for prayer.

This is a natural request from within the community of faith. Christians are to pray for each other. Prayer can become an essential part of the marriage relationship as well.

Some years ago it occurred to me that I was to pray for my family every day. And so, since then, I have prayed for my wife and children every day, twice a day. I also know that I have friends who pray for me each day.

Who but those closest to you know the burdens and issues you face? Who can pray with more compassion and understanding than those who know who and what you are? It ought to be natural for persons in a marriage to pray for each other. But often many fail to do that unless an emergency arises.

Part of the purpose of this devotional experiment is to develop a regular discipline of prayer for each other. Such a practice will become part of the natural rhythm of marriage and invoke God's daily blessing.

Share your thoughts on the meaning and purpose of praying for each other. Are you ready to make such a commitment?

$\mathscr{P}$RAYER

*Lord, teach us to pray. As we journey together in faith and
hope, draw us by Your Holy Spirit into intercessory prayer for
each other. Let our praying mold and shape our love into the
specific prayers and actions that will allow us to enter into the
blessings You have for us. Let us not grow weary in praying
or well doing for each other. In Jesus' name, Amen.*

Share specific prayers for each other.

$\mathscr{J}$OURNALING
Take time to record what seems important to you.

_____

_____

_____

_____

_____

_____

_____

_____

_____

_____

DAY
19

_____
_____
_____
_____
_____
_____
_____
_____
_____
_____
_____
_____
_____
_____

$\mathcal{B}$LESSING

*May I always be allowed to accompany your
thoughts when they turn to God.*

DAY
20

*Live
Together
in the Light*

SILENCE

Light a candle as you share your silence today. In your quiet contemplation seek the light of Christ's presence.

SCRIPTURE

This is the message which we have heard from Him and declare to you, that God is light and in Him is no darkness at all. If we say that we have fellowship with Him, and walk in darkness, we lie and do not practice the truth. But if we walk in the light, as He is in the light, we have fellowship with one another, and the blood of Jesus Christ His Son cleanses us from all sin.

If we say that we have no sin, we deceive ourselves, and the truth is not in us. If we confess our sins, He is faithful and just to forgive us our sins and to cleanse us from all unrighteousness. If we say that we have not sinned, we make Him a liar, and His word is not in us (1 John 1:5–10).

REFLECTION

Nothing builds community and relationships more than honesty about who we are with each other. It is not easy to be honest about the darkness that is part of our lives, and as a result, our relationships are less than they could be.

John writes about walking in the light. Some might interpret his words to mean that you can walk in perfection and never do anything wrong. However, the rest of the passage makes it clear that there is no way you can avoid darkness or sin in your life. The way to move from darkness to light is not by pretending there is no darkness, acting as if you do not sin. The way to light is by admitting your sin and accepting forgiveness for it. As you confess your sins, God forgives and cleanses and puts you in the light.

In the light you can see clearly your need for forgiveness and cleansing. When you are honest about that need, you become free to accept another's love despite what you are. When you can let go of the pretending and freely live in God's and another's acceptance of you with your sin, you move into deep fellowship with God and another.

This deep fellowship is an open, caring, and accepting relationship that is based on the truth and not a deception. You take a leap of great trust admitting to darkness in your life and laying yourself open to another with it. God has promised to respond to such honesty with acceptance and forgiveness. With Christ's love in you, you can give the same acceptance to another.

So many relationships are hindered because of a lack of grace that does not allow another to be honest. Often, even in the church, people pretend they have no sin or inclination to darkness. Such an environment becomes closed, uncaring, and destructive.

Share with each other your struggle to be honest and to live in the light. Share again your promise to accept each other as you are. Let this time become a moment of grace for both of you.

𝒫RAYER

O Christ, You give light to the world because You love and accept us as we are. Send Your Holy Spirit into our hearts so that we may show such grace to each other. Help us to live in the light, trusting that as we acknowledge our darkness, You will cause the light of Your truth to be with us and in us. As You are with us, Christ, give us the courage to walk in Your light, loving and being loved as we are. In Your holy name, Amen.

Add your own prayers or share another time of silence, soaking in God's love for both of you.

JOURNALING

Take time to record what seems important to you.

_____

_____

_____

_____

_____

_____

_____

_____

_____

_____

_____

_____

BLESSING

*May Jesus shine brightly in going before you
and in surrounding you.*

DAY
21

Share
the Same
Treasure

SILENCE

As you enter your silence today, be sensitive to God's love and your love for God above all things. Embrace that love as your greatest treasure and enjoy the gift of its peace.

SCRIPTURE

The kingdom of heaven is like treasure hidden in a field, which a man found and hid; and for joy over it he goes and sells all that he has and buys that field.

Again, the kingdom of heaven is like a merchant seeking beautiful pearls, who, when he had found

one pearl of great price, went and sold all that he had
and bought it (Matt. 13:44–46).

$\mathscr{R}$EFLECTION

In some ways your marriage is similar to these parables. You decided you had found the one person to whom
you wished to give your love and your life. All others
were put aside to devote yourself to this one. Jesus' teaching in these parables may help you see the value of His
presence above all else in your relationship.

Some things are of more value than others. That is
true of your relationship with God in Christ Jesus. This
relationship is the key to understanding and enjoying all
the other people and things in your life. When your relationship with God is straight and given priority, all the
other gifts God has given you will increase in value and
enjoyment, including the gift of each other.

God's presence in your relationship will allow you to
be more for each other rather than less. This is something
of a mystery, but a mystery that is understood by experiencing it.

This devotional life you are developing together will
provide ways in which this mystery can unfold in your
lives. As each puts God first, God will put you first for
each other. The mystery seems to unfold in this way.

Share your reflections and discuss your marriage as a
parable of the kingdom.

*P*RAYER

Open our eyes, O Lord. Open our eyes. Let us behold the treasure of Your presence with us. Let us see clearly the beauty, joy, and faithfulness You bring to us as we honor Your presence in our marriage. Help us to love You above all things. In Jesus' name, Amen.

Add your prayers for yourselves and others.

*J*OURNALING
Take time to record what seems important to you.

_____

_____

_____

_____

_____

_____

_____

_____

_____

_____

_____

_____

_____

_____

_____

_____

_____

_____

_____

_____

_____

_____

_____

_____

_____

_____

_____

$\mathscr{B}$LESSING

*May you always have the wisdom to cherish
the gift of the kingdom of God.*

DAY
22

Amazing Grace

$\mathcal{S}$ILENCE

God loves you and comes to you in full acceptance of who you are. Enter your silence seeking to be touched by that amazing grace.

$\mathcal{S}$CRIPTURE

Therefore, having been justified by faith, we have peace with God through our Lord Jesus Christ, through whom also we have access by faith into this grace in which we stand, and rejoice in hope of the glory of God. And not only that, but we also glory in tribulations, knowing that tribulation produces perseverance; and perseverance, character; and character, hope. Now hope does not disappoint, because the love of God has been poured out in our hearts by the Holy Spirit who was given to us (Rom. 5:1–5).

ℛEFLECTION

Have you ever walked in a bog or swampy area where the ground was moving beneath your feet? You felt uneasy because at any moment you could sink knee-deep in mud. Life can feel that way if nothing solid is underneath you.

Moment by moment your life support can change if you depend only on what others say and think about you. The ground beneath your feet will constantly change if you depend on how other people receive you or judge you. That can be true in your marital relationship as well.

What causes you to affirm or deny each other? The way you act? How the other is meeting your expectations? If so, you walk on swampy ground.

You can take a clue from God. The apostle Paul says, "Through Christ we have obtained access to this grace in which we stand." This grace from God shown to us in Jesus Christ is not based on how we act or don't act. It is not based on whether or not we meet God's expectations. It is presented to us out of God's unconditional love for us. God affirms our worth and value in Christ. In God's grace through Christ, we stand on solid ground. We know where we are with God at all times from the standpoint of God's love for us.

This point of view will bring real stability to your relationship. When you know that your partner loves you because grace-filled love exists in the heart, you are on solid ground.

The apostle goes on to say that this grace enables you to survive suffering and hardship and live in constant hope. When you find yourself evaluating your partner on actions or inactions, met expectations, or how pleasing he or she is, think again of the love that brought you together and the grace that God extends to you.

This grace will enable you to survive differences, difficulties, misunderstandings, and hurts along the way. As you remember the grace of God that is the foundation for your life and relationship, you will renew the strength of the basis of your marriage.

Reflect together on your understanding of this grace that God has given in Christ and how you may help each other to remember it.

𝒫RAYER

O God, we thank You for the infinite variety of Your grace. It is like clear, refreshing, flowing water. It is as frequent and numerous as every moment of each day. It is as solid as granite. In all of these ways and more, let us enjoy the work of Your grace in our lives. Help us remember to feed on this grace each day. In Jesus' name, Amen.

*J*OURNALING

Take time to record what seems important to you.

_____

_____

_____

_____

_____

_____

_____

_____

_____

_____

_____

_____

_____

*B*LESSING

*May you always know a love that comes
with no strings attached.*

DAY
23

Humility

SILENCE

Share your period of silence together. Review the purpose of this silence as explained in the first part of the book. Let it be a time of letting go and seeking to know nothing but the gift of God's presence to you.

SCRIPTURE

He spoke this parable to some who trusted in themselves that they were righteous, and despised others: "Two men went up to the temple to pray, one a Pharisee and the other a tax collector. The Pharisee stood and prayed thus with himself, 'God, I thank You that I am not like other men—extortioners, unjust, adulterers, or even as this tax collector. I fast twice a week; I give tithes of all that I possess.' And the tax collector, standing afar off, would not so much as raise his eyes to heaven, but beat his breast, saying, 'God, be merciful to me a sinner!' I tell you, this man went down to his house justified rather than the other; for everyone who exalts himself will be humbled, and he who humbles himself will be exalted" (Luke 18:9–14).

$\mathcal{R}$EFLECTION

Humility is elusive. Just when you become conscious of having it, it can slip through your fingers. Humility is a state that exists when you are not consciously thinking of your own goodness or achievement. The loss of humility will cause you to forget the common ground on which you stand with all others.

This common ground is the reality that all persons share in weakness and failure. Every person is a sinner before God and must rely on God's forgiveness and acceptance. People are so prone to comparison that they tend to seek to justify their existence by measuring themselves against others.

You separate yourself from others when you put everyone on a different rung on the ladder of goodness. You end up with false pride when doing that becomes a way of life. As the book of Proverbs says, "Pride goes before destruction, and a haughty spirit before a fall" (16:18). For centuries, pride has made it into the Hall of Fame of sins.

The opposite of pride is humility, which is a healthy ingredient for any relationship, but especially for marriage. In humility, you measure yourself against God, not others. In measuring yourself against God, you find yourself standing on the same level as all others. This distinction between pride and humility can serve you well in your relationship.

A piece of advice: seek God's forgiveness each day; forgive yourself each day; forgive each other each day. Each day measure yourself against God and you will be humbled before God and each other.

Discuss your understanding of pride and humility and the way they relate to marriage.

𝒫RAYER

O Jesus Christ, You humbled Yourself and became our servant. You modeled the path of humility as You lived out God's will. Forgive us our foolish pride. Let this pride not be a barrier to our seeing a true perspective of ourselves. Lead us into humility so that we may serve each other well. In Your humble love, hear us. Amen.

𝒥OURNALING

Take time to record what seems important to you.

_____

_____

_____

_____

_____

_____

_____

_____

_____

_____

_____

_____

_____

_____

_____

_____

*B*LESSING

*May God give you the desire and the will
to be what you were meant to be.*

DAY
24

Peace

Silence

Share the silence together. Let go of all that stands in the way of harmony or peace. Let this silence grow longer as you seek a centering in the peace of Christ.

Scripture

Rejoice in the Lord always. Again I will say, rejoice! Let your gentleness be known to all men. The Lord is at hand. Be anxious for nothing, but in everything by prayer and supplication, with thanksgiving, let your requests be made known to God; and the peace of God, which surpasses all understanding, will

guard your hearts and minds through Christ Jesus
(Phil. 4:4–7).

ℛEFLECTION

What is your image of peace? Many people speak of a
total absence of struggle, war, or difference when they
think of peace. This view is idealistic and represents a
wish more than a real-life situation.

Visualize a forest and a beautiful waterfall cascading
down a mountainside. Along with the beauty of such a
scene hear the tremendous roar of sound that is constantly
present. Picture close to the waterfall a tree with a nest and
a young bird in it. The mother bird has just brought home
a worm to eat. The two of them are in the nest enjoying
the feast, content to be safe together. They seem oblivious
to the sound of the waterfall or at least do not seem both-
ered by it. This scene captures the sense of peace described
in the Scripture.

Difficulties will always be present. Struggles will
always exist. There will always be things to tempt you
into anxiety, but even in the midst of them you can find
peace.

The apostle Paul says to take everything to God in
prayer with thanksgiving, and the peace of God will keep
your hearts and minds through Christ Jesus. Prayer is the
secret of peace. It opens a door to the power and care of
God. You can give away the cause of your anxiety and
find peace by releasing it to God. Expressing your fears
and anxieties in prayer together will lead both of you to
contentment and safety in Christ.

With Christ in your nest you can find the release from

anxiety that is pictured in the story of the birds in the forest.

Share your thoughts about this subject.

$\mathscr{P}$RAYER

Gracious God, teach us to offer up everything in our lives with thanksgiving. Deliver us from domination by fear and anxiety. Help us to remember to seek peace in You and Your Son, Jesus. May Your Holy Spirit deepen our trust in Your good care and grace so that we will be free to place all our needs before You. In Jesus' name, Amen.

$\mathscr{J}$OURNALING

Take time to record what seems important to you.

_____

_____

_____

_____

_____

_____

_____

_____

_____

_____

_____

_____

_____

_____

_____

_____

_____

_____

_____

_____

_____

_____

_____

_____

_____

_____

_____

$\mathscr{B}$LESSING

May the peace you receive from God
be the peace that fills each day.

DAY
25

Life in a Crowd

Silence

You may be surprised to learn that entering into personal solitude often enhances awareness of others around you. See what impact your silent time has on your sense of others surrounding you with encouragement and light.

Scripture

Therefore we also, since we are surrounded by so great a cloud of witnesses, let us lay aside every weight, and the sin which so easily ensnares us, and let us run with endurance the race that is set before us, looking unto Jesus, the author and finisher of our faith, who for the joy that was set before Him endured the cross, despising the shame, and has sat down at the right hand of the throne of God (Heb. 12:1–2).

$\mathscr{R}$EFLECTION

"Two's company and three's a crowd," is a saying that attempts to describe the need two people have for intimacy. It also expresses the desire not to have competition from others. In growth toward spiritual intimacy, however, this old adage may not hold true.

It doesn't hold true, first of all, with Christ. The presence of Christ is neither crowding nor competitive. His presence enhances intimacy between two people.

In a spiritual sense a host of others surround you. You are part of an ongoing history of faithful people who found life in relationship with Christ. You are surrounded by a cloud of witnesses (see chapter 11 of Hebrews). They are a testimony of faith-filled living, that is, they lived on the promises of God. These witnesses inspire and encourage your faith journey.

At times going on with your relationship will seem hard. Problems of communication or lack of personal attention may cause you to question your commitment and capacity to continue the relationship. That can happen to any relationship and does not mean it is over. You might need to face some things together and make some changes. Marriage is an ever-changing relationship. This dynamic quality is not necessarily negative. It can work to bring growth and depth to your marriage.

Just as some people blame God for what happens to them and want to bail out when tough times come, so others relate to marriage in the same way. In these times you have to think back to your original commitment and reaffirm your pledge and desire to continue the journey together, knowing that you will endure and will live through it.

Thousands before you have lived faithful and trusting lives together in the face of difficulty, suffering, misunderstanding, and hardship. Like the heroes of faith listed in the Scriptures as a testimony to endurance and faithfulness, countless numbers among family and friends witness to this same endurance in marriage.

Keep looking to the heroes of faith and marriage as an inspiration and encouragement in your journey together. Keep trusting that God is with and for you in this relationship and will not forsake the promises made to you.

Discuss persons who are an inspiration for your marriage. Consider couples among your families and friends. Do you feel a special promise from God for your life together? Share it with each other.

$\mathscr{P}$RAYER

Lord Jesus, pioneer of the faith journey, be the pioneer of our marriage journey as well. Keep us confident in trust and hope in all circumstances. Give us the courage to face changes when they come. Give us honesty to face disagreements. Give us trust to heal all wounds. Help us be open to others who can encourage us. Lord, once again we invite You into our relationship so that Your love can be the strength of our own love. Amen.

Share your prayers with each other.

$\mathcal{J}$OURNALING

Take time to record what seems important to you.

_____

_____

_____

_____

_____

_____

_____

_____

_____

_____

_____

$\mathcal{B}$LESSING

*God bless you with a heart and mind open
to the strength others can give you.*

DAY
26

Timing Is Everything

$\mathcal{S}$ILENCE

In your silence let go of past and future and allow the present moment to be filled with God. Seek wisdom for this moment in your silence with God.

$\mathcal{S}$CRIPTURE

To everything there is a season,
    A time for every purpose under heaven:
A time to be born,
    And a time to die;
A time to plant,
    And a time to pluck what is planted;

A time to kill,
And a time to heal;
A time to break down,
And a time to build up;
A time to weep,
And a time to laugh;
A time to mourn,
And a time to dance;
A time to cast away stones,
And a time to gather stones;
A time to embrace,
And a time to refrain from embracing;
A time to gain,
And a time to lose;
A time to keep,
And a time to throw away;
A time to tear,
And a time to sew;
A time to keep silence,
And a time to speak;
A time to love,
And a time to hate;
A time of war,
And a time of peace (Eccl. 3:1–8).

REFLECTION

Some theologians have said that Ecclesiastes has a certain sense of fatalism—what will be will be. A very real tension exists between God's will being done as God chooses and our freedom to alter our circumstances. This issue becomes important when we realize that two things are essential in discerning what should happen in a given moment.

On the one hand, we need to know what is going on around us. What is happening? Where do things seem to be going? On the other hand, we need to know what decisions we should make.

These questions can be summed up in the question of timing. What time is it? Is it a time for scattering or gathering up? For reaching out or drawing in? For risking or playing it safe?

In your relationship you will come to many crossroads of decision about your future. Ask yourselves, What time is it? In what direction are things moving? What does God want of us at this moment?

When you list pros and cons regarding decisions, remember to ask the timing question. As you do, you will sense what is appropriate for this time. Life has rhythm. There are times of advance and times of retreat; times of activity and times of rest; times of growth and times of pulling in.

Your relationship will benefit from your sense of timing. Take the timing question into your prayer life and your solitude. Let your awareness of timing grow with your spiritual journey.

Share your ideas about the question of timing in your relationship.

$\mathscr{P}$RAYER

O God, help us in the ebb and flow of life to discern Your will. Let us not flounder on the ocean without true direction or purpose. Keep us mindful of Your will and our lives coming together so that we may live in the peace and harmony You

*give. Keep us from willful self-destruction, and guide us with
Your spirit to the creative life to which You have called
us to live together. In Jesus' name, Amen.*

Share your prayer concerns.

$\mathcal{J}$OURNALING

Take time to record what seems important to you.

_____

_____

_____

_____

_____

_____

_____

_____

$\mathcal{B}$LESSING

*May the Holy Spirit give you wisdom to
know the purpose for each moment of time.*

DAY
27

*Love
and
Freedom*

$\int$ILENCE

As you move into your silence, imagine all the weight and barriers that you feel in your life falling away from you. Seek God as a free person in your stillness.

$\int$CRIPTURE

For you were called to freedom, brothers and sisters; only do not use your freedom as an opportunity for self-indulgence, but through love become slaves to one another. For the whole law is summed up in a single commandment, "You shall love your neighbor as yourself." If, however, you bite and devour one another, take care that you are not consumed by one another (Gal. 5:13–15 NRSV).

ℛEFLECTION

Freedom is a wonderful but difficult experience for us humans. We tend to lean to one side or the other of freedom and lose its real blessing.

You may be afraid of freedom and cling to an established path, a set of rules or habits so that you will not have to risk too much. Or you may feel that for freedom's sake you have no boundaries whatsoever.

What gives both boundaries and excitement to freedom? In the Scripture the answer is love. God loves you as you are. Love frees you to risk being you for another.

The boundaries to freedom come in the love that you give and receive from another. For love's sake or that person's sake, you will not want to live out a selfish desire that may hurt.

Love directs this path between license and legalism, and the path is freedom. Love will enable you to live beyond frozen habit or fearful legalism. Love will enable you to live within boundaries that show respect and care and do not abuse the relationship to which you are committed.

Living beyond habit or legalism frees you to be who you are so that you can be a real and responsive human being. Living with boundaries frees you to live responsibly in love so that you do not hurt the other.

Discuss your sense of freedom and boundaries in your relationship.

*P*RAYER

*Lord Jesus, You have set us free by Your love and for Your love.
Guide us by Your spirit to live in that glorious free space
between legalism and license. Show us when to risk and
when to hold back. Give us a true spirit of discernment
of the boundaries of Your love so that we do not hurt
each other. In Your name we pray, dear Lord, Amen.*

*J*OURNALING

Take time to record what seems important to you.

_____

_____

_____

_____

_____

_____

_____

_____

_____

_____

_____

_____

_____

_____

_____

_____

_____

_____

_____

_____

_____

_____

_____

_____

_____

_____

_____

_____

ℬLESSING

*May God's love break the chains of fear
and guilt so that you may enjoy
fully His love and mine.*

DAY
28

Abundant Life

$\mathcal{S}$ILENCE

Continue to seek an emptiness within yourself, letting go of control, thoughts, and self-centeredness. Allow God to fill the empty spaces.

$\mathcal{S}$CRIPTURE

Jesus said to them again, "Most assuredly, I say to you, I am the door of the sheep. All who ever came before Me are thieves and robbers, but the sheep did not hear them. I am the door. If anyone enters by Me, he will be saved, and will go in and out and find pasture. The thief does not come except to steal, and to kill, and to destroy. I have come that they may have life, and that they may have it more abundantly. I am the good shepherd. The good shepherd gives His life for the sheep" (John 10:7–11).

$\mathscr{R}$EFLECTION

There is life, and then there is Life. Jesus says that there are those who promise life but only steal, kill, and destroy. A lot of con artists are at work in the world. Many make promises but only to take advantage. They care nothing for others.

Jesus declares Himself to be the good shepherd who gives His life for the sheep. He is also the door, or gate, of the sheepfold, guarding the flock and leading them to green pastures. Jesus functions as both the means of salvation—laying down His life for us—and the way to abundant life—guiding and blessing our lives. As your life is lived in Christ, you are enabled to live in the wisdom of Christ, discerning good and evil.

The key phrase is, "As your life is lived in Christ." Like any person, you can be deceived by others and yourself. No matter how educated or sophisticated you are, you face obstacles like sin, illusion, and compulsions that cloud your ability to make good decisions.

A wisdom comes to you from your Creator through Jesus Christ that leads through these obstacles. This wisdom comes to you primarily through the Scriptures. Christian fellowship, prayer, and other means of keeping in touch with Christ will add to your spiritual growth in wisdom. Such wisdom will direct you to the abundant life.

Abundant life is more a matter of wisdom than the accumulation of things. In our culture this idea may be difficult to accept. As you live out your life together, however, this reality will become more and more clear to you.

Discuss your shared vision of the abundant life.

𝒫RAYER

Jesus, Good Shepherd, guide and direct our lives in the path of wisdom. We do want to know the abundant life You have promised. Keep us, O Lord, from those things that will rob us of life and lead us astray. Save and guide us, gracious Shepherd. Amen.

Share your prayers for your needs today.

𝒥OURNALING

Take time to record what seems important to you.

_____

_____

_____

_____

_____

_____

_____

_____

_____

_____

_____

_____

_____

_____

_____

_____

_____

_____

_____

_____

_____

_____

_____

_____

_____

_____

ℬLESSING

*God bless you with abundant life through
your trust in the wisdom of Jesus Christ.*

DAY
29

A Big Decision

SILENCE

Share your silence holding hands. This touch may be distracting at first, but let it pass. Focus on silence, stillness, and solitude. Follow your breathing in and out, and seek a still point where God's presence can be felt.

SCRIPTURE

Now therefore, fear the LORD, serve Him in sincerity and in truth, and put away the gods which your fathers served on the other side of the River and in Egypt. Serve the LORD! And if it seems evil to you to serve the LORD, choose for yourselves this day whom you will serve, whether the gods which your fathers served that were on the other side of the River, or the gods of the Amorites, in whose land you dwell. But as for me and my house, we will serve the LORD (Josh. 24:14–15).

$\mathscr{R}$EFLECTION

Joshua, nearing the end of his life, challenges the people he has led into the Promised Land with a big decision. He calls on them to decide which god they will serve. He reminds them of the Lord's blessings and protection. He reminds them of the way God has promised to be with them always. But he knows the human tendency to respond to other gods. He makes his own pledge of faithfulness for himself and his household and challenges the others to do the same.

God has brought you together and blessed you with your marriage covenant and all the gifts that surround your life together. In the days ahead you will be tempted to put other things before God. Many distractions will call for your attention and allegiance. You may even be tempted to think that you can go it alone without God. There will be times when it seems that you are really putting it together yourselves. Life will come easy on those days. You may forget God.

Joshua's challenge remains for every household in the Christian community. Being faithful takes a commitment made over and over again.

Your journey through these devotional exercises has opened up for you the blessings a deepening relationship with God and with each other in Christ can bring. Your journey in Scripture, reflection, and prayer has brought an exciting dimension to your married life. As you continue in a devotional life together, your commitment to serve God will be sustained and strengthened.

Discuss the ways in which your Christian commitment can be sustained and lived out in your relationship. What pitfalls are you aware of that could diminish your commitment?

RAYER

O God, You have created us to walk with You under the blessing of Your hand. By the Holy Spirit, give us strength to live each day committed to love and allegiance toward You. Keep us from things that draw us away from You, and lead us to things that will bind our hearts to Yours. Make us ever aware of the dangers of false allegiance, and deliver us from thinking of ourselves as sufficient without You. In Jesus' name, Amen.

Continue with your own prayers.

OURNALING

Take time to record what seems important to you.

_____

_____

_____

_____

_____

_____

_____

_____

_____

_____

_____

_____

_____

_____

_____

ℬLESSING

*The Holy Spirit bless you with strength to
renew your decision to love me each day.*

DAY
30

Where Does It All End?

SILENCE

"Be still, and know that I am God" (Ps. 46:10). Let your silence lead you to this knowledge.

SCRIPTURE

And I heard, as it were, the voice of a great multitude, as the sound of many waters and as the sound of mighty thunderings, saying, "Alleluia! For the Lord God Omnipotent reigns! Let us be glad and rejoice and give Him glory, for the marriage of the Lamb has come, and His wife has made herself ready."

117

Then he said to me, "Write: 'Blessed are those who
are called to the marriage supper of the Lamb!'" And
he said to me, "These are the true sayings of God"
(Rev. 19:6–7, 9).

$\mathscr{R}$EFLECTION

In the Bible, descriptions of God and God's activity
are often pictured in images that describe our common
life. In the book of Revelation the image of a marriage
supper is used to describe the great reunion of Christ and
His people. Those faithful ones become the bride of the
Lamb, who was slain for the sins of the world.

No doubt you remember your wedding reception or
dinner. It may be a bit of a blur because of the emotion of
the moment and the bustle of activity. However, you can
probably recall your feelings of joy and excitement. The
days of planning and preparation were over. Families and
friends were gathered to share in your commitment and in
anticipation of your married life together.

The description of our ultimate ending in the glory of
God's heaven is much like the marriage feast that you remember. Eternal life with God and the Lamb will be like
that great celebration of joy and excitement. Life will be
fulfilled.

In this life, anticipation of something grander and
more wonderful always lies ahead of you. You continue to
live toward a future that holds greater mystery and joy
than you have known. Your marriage can be a journey
that moves toward that ultimate experience of community
with God and God's faithful ones in an everlasting marriage feast. Your life together can be the means of

strengthening your bonds with God's grace in Christ as you live together in God's Word, sacrament, and faith relationship through the Holy Spirit.

Each little or big celebration of your marriage can be a reminder of the great celebration toward which you are living together—the marriage feast of the Lamb.

Think about choosing a symbol that would serve as a reminder of that great feast to come. It could be a picture, a saying, or something you write and put in a prominent place in your home. Discuss ways you can keep this vision alive in your marriage.

$\mathscr{P}$RAYER

O Lamb of God, You are the beginning and the end. Help us to make our journey with You that we may enjoy forever the gift of Your gracious presence. Without You we will never know the depths of true joy and community. With You we will live forever in joys that we cannot even imagine. Keep before us the vision of the marriage feast that has no end that we may be pulled forward in all circumstances toward the marvelous continuation of abundant life forever. Amen.

Add your own prayers of hope for the future.

$\mathscr{J}$OURNALING

Take time to record what seems important to you.

_____

_____

_____

_____

_____

_____

_____

_____

_____

_____

_____

_____

_____

_____

_____

_____

ℬLESSING

May the end of our loving days be as
beautiful as the beginning as we
share the feast of love.

CLOSING
WORDS

*Y*ou have been on a journey of sorts: silence, Scripture, reflection, prayer, remembering—all have been a part of what you have been sharing. What has happened to you, you alone can say.

You have experienced what works for both of you in sharing a devotional time that leads to a deeper spiritual intimacy. And Jesus has been present to you as promised when you gathered in His name.

You can use other devotional books and, of course, the Bible as you continue to share a devotional time. A conversation with your pastor or spiritual director may be helpful in continuing with new material or deepening aspects of these exercises.

In whatever way you decide to continue, a disciplined pattern of spiritual growth for your marriage relationship will be significant for you.

Along the way, change and variety will be needed. Stay alert to those times.

Last, continue to claim the rich promise of Jesus that "where two or three are gathered together in My name, I am there in the midst of them" (Matt. 18:20).

RECOMMENDED READING

Baldwin, Christina. *One to One: Self-Understanding Through Journal Writing*. New York: M. Evans & Co., 1977.

Bloom, Anthony. *Beginning to Pray*. New York: Paulist Press, 1970.

Kelsey, Morton T. *Adventure Inward: Christian Growth Through Personal Journal Writing*. Minneapolis, Minn.: Augsburg, 1980.

Kiersey, David, and Marilyn Bates. *Please Understand Me: Character and Temperament Types*. Del Mar, Calif.: Prometheus Nemesis Books, 1984.

Michael, Chester, and Norissey, Marie. *Prayer and Temperament*. Charlottesville, Va.: Open Door, Inc., 1984.

Nouwen, Henry J. M. *Reaching Out: Three Movements of the Spiritual Life*. Garden City, N.Y.: Doubleday, 1975.

———. *With Open Hands*. Notre Dame, Ind.: Ave Maria Press, 1972.

Pennington, Basil M. *Centering Prayer*. New York: Image Books, 1982.

Rinker, Rosalind. *Prayer: Conversing with God*. Grand Rapids, Mich.: Zondervan, 1959.

Sandford, John A. *Between People: Communicating One-to-One*. Ramsey, N.J.: Paulist Press, 1982.